TREASURES

a compilation

by the YMCA Lincoln Park Senior
Center Writers Group

ISBN# 978-1-7323637-7-9

For additional copies of this work, please contact:

Doodle and Peck Publishing
P.O. Box 852105
Yukon, OK 73085
(405) 354-7422

Book design by Marla F. Jones
Fonts used: Algerian, Anna, and AR Blanca

Dedicated to Adella Smith
1932 - 2018

Miss Adorable Adella kept us thinking of others and how we could make a difference. As I listened to her stories of growing up in Oklahoma City, I quickly realized she was more than adorable, she was a gem. Her sharp wit and her unexpected humorous quips kept us eager for more. We will miss you forever.

Gwendolyn Hooks

My deepest and heartfelt sympathy to the family of Adella Smith, your loved one. I knew her as a teacher, counselor, and a Christian lady. May God give you courage to accept her homegoing.

Georgia Juniper

Your life wrote a joyful story, full of light and beauty. Thanks for your words and music. Your children and the Ambassador Choir rise up to sing your praise.

Norma Noble

Thanks for sharing beautiful tidbits of your life with the class. You really showed you cared. You said your grandmother called you a big mouth because you told on everybody. I suppose you're going to be busy telling God about us which will make him laugh.

Joyce Tease Jackson

I hereby dedicate to the one and only Adorable Adella, the writings from our times together in our Senior Writers Group. You helped to make it fun and memorable.

Lynnette "The Poette" Hodge

I was sorry to hear of your passing, but the Lord knows best. He was ready for you to come home. We will meet our Lord one day and see you again.

Psalm 147:3 - He healeth the broken in heart, and bindeth up their wounds.
I'm praying for your family and I love you and miss you.
Queen Esther Sattiewhite

Some say it takes a life time to get to know someone. But when a person is straight forward and to the point, all it takes is an instant. I met you once; but your presence will be forever felt, through the stories you've shared and memories of those who loved most. Rest well Miss Adella, you're in the best hands now.
Bertil Jerrie Hooks

3

TABLE OF CONTENTS

COLOR SLIDES

FOREWORD

In the fall of 2015, All Access Arts – Arts Council Oklahoma City asked me to teach a writing class at the YMCA Lincoln Park Senior Center. I soon realized, I would not be a teacher. My role was facilitator. Three of the ladies were the authors of published poetry books. They were all career women, most with college degrees, including masters. They were world travelers. Life choices sent one to live in Washington, DC and then Delaware.

The group includes writers from Texas, Tennessee, and Oklahoma. Some are farm girls, some city chicks. One still loves to dance and it's easy to imagine her heating up the dance floor at her Texas high school. One lady sewed her school clothes on a Singer with a knee pedal. Another rode a city bus to school from her home west of downtown to the northeast side of Oklahoma City. It was the only school open to her, and she was determined to become an educated lady and educate those who would follow her.

Despite our various careers, we love the process of writing as a way to remember. I soon realized the stories were so fascinating and full of life, they deserved to be collected and shared. This book is a compilation of lives well-lived and living.

Gwendolyn Hooks

BERTIL JERRIE HOOKS

Bertil Jerrie Hooks is a Louisiana native. She was born in New Orleans, Louisiana, but likes to say that she is from both Louisiana and Oklahoma, since she moved to the of state of Oklahoma in her early teens. Bertil is a wife, mother, grandmother and great-grandmother. She co-pastors a church with her husband in a small community called Crescent, Oklahoma.

Her hobbies are walking, fishing, and watching westerns. She also enjoys journaling. Bertil credits her writings as a significant part of a healing process through the death of her Mother. She dreams to publish some of her writings and hopes to one day write a biography.

Digging Deep to Find the Treasure in You While Putting Self in Self-Esteem

Google defines self-esteem as "being confident in one's own worth or abilities; self-respect." Some of the synonyms for self-esteem are self-respect, pride, dignity, self-regard, and faith in one-self.

What happens when self is taken away from esteem? Self is defined as a person's essential being that distinguishes them from others, especially considered as the object of introspection or reflexive action.

Esteem is defined as respect and admiration, typically for a person. The synonyms for esteem are respect, admire, value, regard, acclaim, appreciate, like, prize, treasure, favor, revere.

The journey of discovering my self-worth has been long and sometimes challenging. It takes a whole lot of questions: acknowledgment, confessions and some deep soul searching to figure out that you have lost the self out of esteem. My Mother used to say, "When a person gets sick and tired of something, that's when you see a change".

I had battled depression for many years. Not understanding when or why it was happening. I just became sick and tired of depression one day. I got tired of always feeling alone no matter who was with me. I got tired of the days of the quietness and the suicidal thoughts in my mind. So I went on a journey to discover exactly what was going on with myself. I went on a journey to get the answers that the doctors with all their pills and questions couldn't help me.

I scuba dived into my soul. If you're not familiar with scuba diving, google defines scuba diving as "being a mode of underwater diving where the diver uses a self-contained underwater breathing apparatus which is completely independent of surface supply, to breathe underwater."

You get to see those things that are impossible to see on the surface. I began to do a lot of writing. I began by trying to recall my childhood. I was surprised to discover I only had a couple of vivid memories at the age of six. One pleasant and one not so pleasant. Then I went to my adolescent years. I was able to discover a memory that I believe changed my life for what I believe at the time was forever.

Then I went on to my teenage years. I didn't realize at the time that the trauma that had taken place during my adolescent years had set the stage for my teenage years. Like a scuba diver I dug deep and I didn't stop digging until I found the source. And once I found the source, unknowingly to me, I was on a journey to rediscovering myself, my true self.

The process of scuba diving is quite interesting, to receive your certification process, it has to be part of an Open Water Course, it involves three main elements; basic knowledge and review, pool skills and equipment evaluation and open water. I found that to be quite interesting as I went on a journey to find myself. The open water to me represents my life. The basic knowledge and review is how much do I really know about myself. Exactly, why do I think the way I think.

Well, by now you get the picture as to why I chose to equate scuba diving with getting in touch with myself. Digging deep within myself, I found a lot of issues that played a huge part as to why I had experienced depression for so many years. These treasures that I found not only helped me with understanding depression; but it also, helped me to understand my past anxiety, panic attacks and low self-esteem.

Going deep not only helped me to discover the root but it helped me to heal in areas that I thought were impossible to heal. How do you put self back in esteem? You find it by digging deep within yourself and finding the source of what caused you to lose self-respect, pride, dignity, self-regard, faith in yourself.

If you're familiar with a tree, you know roots stretch far and wide to give trees a stable foundation. So, does history. Things that happened in our past plays a significant part in our lives. Good or bad, our past is our foundation. Depending on what happened in your past-in my case several traumas-how you live your present life.

My story deals with self-esteem issues. With mental illness being on the rise in this country, you have to ask yourself, why isn't there anything being done about it?

Some people are choosing to live their lives free from any traumatic experience they've suffered in life. Some chose to mask the hurts of their past and cover it with careers, money, relationships, trips, cars, houses etc. We often ask ourselves when we hear of a entertainer or someone we viewed as successful, why did they kill themselves or why did they go crazy? Because in many cases they refuse to deal with deep issues of their past.

The greatest gift we can give ourselves in life is the gift of health. We owe it to ourselves to be healthy in mind; body and soul. In the bible, Paul says it this way, 3 John 1:2 Beloved, I pray that you may prosper and enjoy good health, as your soul also prospers. Putting the self in esteem requires healing. A healing in every area of your mind, body and soul. Sometimes we have to go scuba diving to get to the bottom of those matters of the heart that stops us from being truly great. Not just on the outside but on the inside as well.

Life happens. Divorce, death, lost employment, weight gain and weight lost, disfigurements, rape, lost of businesses, failed ideas etc. These things take a little from us each time. And every time we're faced with another disappointment it adds to the first disappointment, which slowly eats away and separates self from esteem.

This journey of repairing my self-esteem lead me to long ago suppressed memories. It led me to hurts I thought didn't matter. It led me through emotions I didn't understand but was willing to go through to be free. It lea me to a truth that told me I was living a lie. It led me to a conversation I had with myself. It lead me to a hope that produced great joy. Scuba diving into my heart led to the pains of my past, which was the root. It allowed me to dig up the root of what caused me to lose the self part of self-esteem. Dealing with my past brought me healing and out of that healing I found the treasures of authenticity. I found my true self. Now, I have self-esteem.

The Day I Saw Heaven

Wow! Look how tall! Look like they go all the way up to the sky! SOOO pretty! I remember these words even today, words I spoke to my godfather as we topped a hill entering the state of Florida. The trip was so long and I was so tired of sitting in the back of his truck. I was only 8 years old and the equivalent time hadn't registered to me yet. My godfather was a professional landscaper. He delivered plants and flowers to many states.

This trip I just happened to be out of school and he asked my Mom if I could go. I was so excited! Mind you, I had no idea that this trip would be so long.

As I climbed into this big truck it was like climbing up an eight feet ladder. The seat was so far away from the ground. As I sat in the truck I began to look around, it was intimidating; all the knobs and gadgets were unlike anything I had ever seen in an automobile.

Suddenly, I heard a voice that startled me! "Looking out for that black cat sitting on the east side of the street -10:4." The different sounds and hisses was somewhat alarming. I later found out that the voice from the talking box was a trucker traveling along the same highway we would be traveling, warning my godfather about a police car on the side of the road.

Needless to say; this trip was a trip of a life time. Loud voices, bumpy roads, one-minute sunshine, the next rain, one-minute hot and the next cold and then hot again. It felt like I went to sleep ten times.

Suddenly, it was all worth it! The beauty of the perfectly blue waters, the white sand, and the flowers! Every color you can imagine was on that beach. The trees stood tall with their leaves fanning as if they were welcoming you to their beautiful city. The flowers all appear to be smiling as if they were saying, "you're going to enjoy your stay here." Even the air had an aroma of a sweet order. It was an amazing experience! One I will always remember as, "The day I saw Heaven."

GEORGIA P. JUNIPER

Georgia P. Juniper was born Georgia Ethelyn Perry in Mansfield, Tennessee. She was the seventh of eight children born to Elmus and Lucinda Perry, who lived on a small farm. Grandmother Mary, who lived with them, used the Blue Back Speller to teach Georgia the alphabet.

Georgia attended a rural elementary school, where she completed the eighth grade. She then took a ten mile bus ride to attend Central High School. She finished in 1952 as salutatorian of her graduation class. She enrolled at Lane College in Jackson, Tennessee, where she majored in elementary education with a minor in social studies. Georgia graduated with the honor of cum laude and began her teaching career in 1956.

Her first job was in a room school in Saulsbury, Tennessee, called Pleasant Hill. After one year of teaching, she moved to Washington, D.C. and lived with her sister. She soon landed a teaching position. She recited a variety of poems before classes began and during school assemblies. She also shared poetry in the Bible classes she taught.

Georgia married James R. Juniper in 1958, and his duties with the United States (USAF) moved them to Dover, Delaware. She completed a certification in special education at the University of Delaware and taught in that field for three years. The USAF moved the Junipers to Oklahoma City in 1964. Georgia completed a master's degree in education with a focus on reading from Central State University, now called the University of Central Oklahoma. The last of her 35 years teaching was for Oklahoma City Public Schools, and the children in those class rooms benefited from her poetry recitations.

Georgia is the mother of three sons, Andre, Alan and Aaron. She is a grandmother and a great grandmother. She is actively involved in Phi Delta Kappa Sorority, an educators association, through which she teaches social skills, crafts and writing to high school girls. She has been a member of the Church of Christ or over 60 years. Georgia's poetry has been published in newspapers, church bulletins, anthologies and at www.poetry.com. *Poems and Inspirations* is her first book.

Changed Perspective

My sister, Alma, is an early riser and enjoys getting up early in the quiet moments before her family would wake up. She would use this time to read the bible, pray, and write to her family members to encourage them to study God's word. She awakened one morning and settled into her favorite chair with a hot cup of coffee. She was confronted by an untidy mess left by her husband, who had failed to clean up after watching a boxing game the night before. Alma became distracted at first and her frustration with her husband took away the pleasure of the moment.

Then a thought came to her to move outside to the patio. From there she could observe the rising of the morning sun, birds feeding on their favorite food, beautiful flowers and gray squirrels scurrying up and down the tall oak trees. The beauty of the scene God painted that morning changed her prospective.

When she told her husband the story, they both understood the lesson of the morning. We do have a choice to accept or not to accept the things that may control or impact our day. We can continue to let the mess frustrate us or we can change our perspective.

When my sister and her husband departed for work that morning, her husband was inspired to change his perspective too. He decided to let the Lord help him to see his messes through her eyes and His.

———————————

Dear Lord, give me the strength to change our perspective rather than linger over messes. Help us to see and fix the "messes" we make for others.

———————————

Philippians 4:13

14

Leaving You in the Hands of the Lord

In 1952, on the morning when I left home for my freshman year to attend Lane College, my mother went off to work as the "HELP" for fifty cents an hour. She bid me good-bye and said," Georgia, I'm leaving you in the hands of the Lord".

My dad was in the veteran's hospital in Nashville, Tennessee to be treated for stomach problems. I was churning milk for butter. After I completed my chore, I carefully wrapped a towel around the churn of fresh buttermilk and butter, called a cab, and went to the bus station a half mile away. This began my journey of really being away from my devoted and loving family.

If we keep our minds focused on the Lord's commands, we will have smooth travels. Mom knew that I was moving into maturity and needed guidance all the way despite what I would encounter.

Stay in the hands of God.

My Grandmother's Apron

Each morning she wrapped it around her waist,
And tied the strings with the least of haste.
She used her apron to lift hot pots from the wood stove,
And to cuddle a baby with the greatest of love.
She used it as a holder after gathering eggs
And when near the fireplace to shield her legs.
It was used to swipe a buzzing bee or an annoying fly,
To clean a plate or a tear to dry.
We snuck behind it when company came for a safe place
And for security to cover our shy face.
It came in handy to warm her arms,
And to drape her shoulders like a cape adorned.
It often was a carrier for chips and kindling for the cast iron stove,
Or to dust furniture and the mantle above.
Fruit and veggies nestled in it at harvest time.
It even was used to give golden apples a sparkling shine.
So if you thought its usefulness not quite enough?
Its large pocket held her money and Burton Snuff.

Genesis 3:7 And the eyes of them were both opened, and they knew that they were both naked; and they sewed leaves together, and made themselves aprons.

NORMA NOBLE

Born in Victoria, Texas to Benjamin Walter and Nettie Ethel Noble, Norma spent a happy childhood in this small south Texas community. She moved with her family to Muskogee, Oklahoma when her father was called to pastor the historic Antioch Baptist Church. She is a proud graduate of the Manual Training High School class of 1960. Her Texas and Oklahoma roots frame the context of many of her life reflections.

Norma attended Texas Southern University, Northeastern State University and the University of Oklahoma receiving B.A. and MEd degrees in French and English and a MA in Human Relations. After teaching several years in Muskogee, she worked in Oklahoma City as Deputy Director of the Human Resources Department and Administrative Coordinator/Utilities Superintendent. She was Director of the Oklahoma County One-Stop Center (Oklahoma's first) and ended her career as Deputy Secretary of the Oklahoma Department of Commerce for Workforce Development and Executive Director of the Oklahoma Workforce Investment Board.

Noble has a life-long avocation in music. She has been Minister of Music for the Evangelistic Baptist Church of Christ since 1973. She has served as music coordinator at the state, region and national convention levels. She is a member and assistant director of the Ambassadors' Concert Choir. She is also the co-director of the Ambassadors' Children and Youth Choir. In addition to board service for the Ambassadors', she is a member of the Regional Food Bank, NTu, A+Oklahoma, K20 and Corporation for a Skilled Workforce Boards of Directors.

Music and Me

MUSIC makes me smile. Music is such an ingrained part of me. I want to sing, "THIS IS ME". It's in my bones, my marrow, in my head and nerve endings—my genes. Its feeling and tingling and heart and vision---strength. Yes---smiles.

Part of my music juice flows from my Dad, Benjamin. Not the Rev. Dr. Noble. No, enter Ben, the singer, dancer, showman, music theatre—vaudevillian. Later, there was Ben the college music minor, pageant/playwright; chorister, choir director, solo artist, music promoter and pulpiteer. The Ben that wanted me to be an opera singer is there, but that's another story.

Then there is the Nettie juice. That's my Mom, mother, sister girl---long before she was a Sis. Noble, First Lady/Pastor's wife. In 1937 she was a basketball star, ACE student, toe tapping, rhythmic, humming, slow dancing, head swagging, YEAH! Music is a mind thing. Music feeds the soul, pushes the meaning. Be still, my soul. Nettie always smiled when she was listening to music. (Me, too.)

Then there is Zan, my cousin Zandever, who played professional xylophone like Lionel Hampton in the recording I was hearing. Cousin Zan crossed the music divide of church and blues. Zan always stayed at our house when he came to town---Victoria, TX. These were pre-Pastor Noble days. Most of our relatives stayed with us—some for a few nights; some for a few weeks or months. Whatever was needed was accommodated.

Zan could really play. But he never played in bands or clubs in Victoria, his home town. He came to Victoria between 'gigs'. Sooo, he could play his xylophone at church---The Palestine Baptist Church. He would play "Just a Closer Walk" or one of the hymn adaptation (not too 'dapted'). All of the righteous folk would sway their heads and smile and toe tap and pretend that they didn't know that Zan played 'the devil's music' or that Tommy Dorsey didn't also write "Tight Like That".

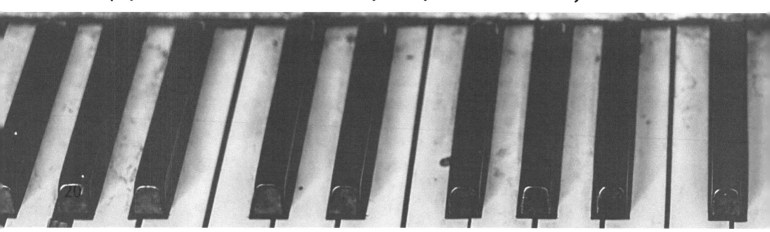

They would give Cousin Zan a few quarters or a tip on a short term job until his next gig would roll up. And he would play all kinds of music at our house. It would be the house of music while he was there—soulful music, never sinful.

There was always music at our house---singing and playing in the day and "Randy the Record man" at night. My dad rehearsed his male chorus at the house. He and my brother prepared their song and dance act for productions. We had a functional, tuned piano so Billy Barefield and Charles Sander came over to play. Billy went on to play in the Air Force and for churches across the nation during his military career. Charles Sanders (Boy Blue) finished the Cleveland Conservatory of Music and eventually went on to become the managing editor and writer for Johnson Publications. He covered Dr. King's Nobel Prize award in Sweden and ran the Paris office for Ebony and Jet for three years. He wrote the Paris and Europe music scenes for Jet during the heyday of African Americans in Europe and the beginnings of Pan Africanism. We read his articles and my mother shared letters with his sisters in Victoria.. That was during the days when people wrote letters to really inform (pre-Facebook). Were we proud! When he was in America, he lived in Chicago. He and my dad were life-long friends. The grand 'Boy Blue'.

My music heart and spirit were further honed by Norma Lee Hobbs' hymn and inspirational singing, Mrs. Broadus's 'shades of Alfalfa' solos, my Mother's multigenerational Revival Chorus, Sis. Mary Magdalene's music lessons at the Catholic convent, B. I. Jones' Columbia/New York City-influenced High School choir, Avalon Reece's (school band director) church Youth Choir patterned after the Chicago gospel groups of the fifties: Roberta Martin, the Caravans, the Barrett sisters, Clay Evans, First Church of Deliverance. Stan, my brother, strongly immersed me in jazz and I'm sure it kept me from the 'sins of rock and roll'. My classmate, Pat Reed, had an uncle, Aaron Bell, who played bass for the Modern Jazz Quartet. He had also graduated from our high school. And I had 'Boy Blue'. Hooked! Music---I love music!

The stories and profiles of the musical giants and players contributed a large part in shaping my musical persona. They are just as important as the notes and skills, melodies and musical messages and history. My music is never just experienced as mere notes and pitches. The sounds are always contextualized by the people, their story and their message. I never sang opera the way my father dreamed, but I do love opera and classical music and gospel and jazz and Broadway and spirituals and hymns and folk music...

(After listening to Benny Goodman, Lionel Hampton, and Charlie Christian playing 'FLYING HOME'.)

Why I Write

Why I write? I think I write because I read and enjoyed it so much that I wanted to say something worth reading. This class is the first time I've been encouraged to write freely. Before, I was told to write scripts, pageants and plays etc. but not encouraged to write my thoughts. In school, it was write your opinion of what somebody else wrote. I missed that creative writing class or session. My teachers probably were afraid of what I might write. My father would have agreed with them.

So I am grateful for the many people who have helped me reach this writing project. First, I thank Harriet Broadus, my minister's wife and nursery school teacher, who read to me in her lap when I was 18 months while she was reading to the older kids (four and five year olds). So I learned to read without sight words. I heard and felt the joy, excitement and energy of words in context.

Thank you, Mrs. Broadus. I also acknowledge the contributions of Ruth Green, my seventh grade English teacher, who lovingly taught grammar, language and the science of phrasing.
Kudos to Ms. Redd, our school's 19 year old librarian, who first introduced me to the world of books; and to Charlene Clark who introduced me to African American literature. I thank my many students who grew from my love of books and music and to those brought me and introduced me to new literature that I would probably have never found.

I acknowledge my multi-talented kids: Pat Piercy and Darryl Riley, Ezelmo Stephens(Opio Toure), my 1971 Muskogee sophomore English class (Judges, engineers, labor activists, doctors, ---beautiful people who still love books and music and life; to Marge Goldstein and Sandy ----, the first white people I had met who were and are pure in heart; to my family Nettie (a writer) and Ben Noble, my parents, my brother Stan, the wonderful encourager, Cousin Pat, brothers Patrick Smith and Hersey Hammons and my kids---Armetta Murphy, Sandra Thompson, Cheryl Gibson, Dennis Scott, Melvin Wallace and my God-son, Vincent Wallace.
Thank you Dr. George Henderson for letting me observe good writing as it was evolving. Finally, I am grateful to this writing class for the opportunity to learn and grow and share.

Monday Morning Musings

      I never thought it would happen. But, I always wanted to write about some of the craziness of my past: the 'strangies' I've encountered, the peaks and valleys of my journey, my dreams and nightmares and the events that brought them to light.

However, I could never seem to get the thoughts on paper. Minnie Vickers had me record my 'story'/my dad's story as a part of the NPR Story book project. That signaled that it might be fun to try to write some of the stories. But I never did.

      Then, these ladies invited me to their writing group that met Monday mornings after our exercise class at the Senior Center. Although I didn't know any of them, their introductions were warm, inviting. The class process was simple. We were given a topic or as in that first day, we listened to a recording and were told to write afterward.

Write what? Write what I thought about during the song. What did the music, rhythm or lyrics, make me feel or think and why? It worked. I had had feeling and thoughts. I wrote them; and I had fun!

      Wonder of wonders, after we finished writing we were encouraged---bullied---into reading what we had written. WHOA! I repeat, I didn't know these women. My thoughts were personal. But, I trusted them just enough to try to softly read my musing.

They were accepting and encouraging. So, I came back and continued to come with great anticipation to my Monday Morning Musings sessions. I hope my kids will read some of them someday and appreciate that their Mom was indeed---CRAZY! But that in spite of that, they will know that God has been gracious in using me in His service and that I have had fun along the way.

Our Hair

My hair---oh, there were the three pigtails: one sticking up in the front, the other two in the back, sorta. Not pretty, just not 'all over you head!'

"I'll comb it". 'Did you get those kinky beads?!' 'You hurt!" Don't comb out the kinks without brushing it first. Of course, there wasn't always a brush. Your mother had a brush which she also used for spanking. You, little girl, had a wide-toothed comb. It was not the same. Put some Royal Crown on it.

Then, on a special occasion (sometimes for Sunday), Mother would 'straighten' my hair on Saturday night. Of course in south Texas it was hot and we sweat, sweat--not just perspire. And, my hair would 'go back' before we could get to church on Sunday morning.

Mrs. Hodge was the mother of Barbara Ann, my classmate, and her sisters Velma Ray and Carolyn. Because she had girls she was sensitive to girls and hair and pain. She knew how to relax me/us and maneuver around the curves and bumps in my nobleian head without taking me in for first degree burns.

In Victoria, we could have chosen to go to Sis. Choice, another hair dresser. She was married to Elder Choice, pastor of the Church of God in Christ. We used to stand outside their little church, watching their services through the windows. I had seen Sis. Choice bucking and rolling around on the floor. She could really dress. But, I didn't trust her to hallelujah on my head.

Then there was Mrs. Purdy. Mrs. Purdy was kin to the "evil one". She belonged to our church but didn't attend much. She didn't seem to like anyone. She never smiled. And, when you were in her chair, she'd jerk your head and body around. She would say, "hold your ear" while the hot comb sizzled. Then, she would burn your hand.

The pains of nappy hair continued from Texas to Oklahoma. I went to Ms. Mattie McPherson's beauty shop in Muskogee. She was a member of my father's church. But she was just as mean as Mrs. Purdy. This observation did much to debunk my life observation that meanness went with un-churched light-skinned people's (like Mrs. Purdy) behavior toward darker people.

Mattie McPherson was "blacker than a hundred midnights" but just as mean and cantankerous. Mattie also cursed a lot and jerked your head a lot harder. The jerks were pinpoints in her narratives. She wasn't talking to me or about me. She just talked, and talked and cussed.

She made her own hair dressing, that's grease. Some of the ingredients didn't completely dissolve.

Soooo, when the hot comb hit these bits, they would 'pop' open and fry your hair and scalp and Mattie's fingers which made her cuss more and jerk your head (my head).

I wasn't saved by the natural or afro until after I had finished college and was teaching in the high school where I had grown up.   Of course, since I went to an all-black school, afros were not allowed. We sent kids home who tried to wear them.

My dad tried to stay 'neutral 'in his opinions to me by saying, you should "try to look pretty". Rev. Crain's wife was much more blunt. Rev. Crain was dad's father in the ministry so her opinion was important. She declared, "That a woman's hair was her glory" thus saith the Lord. Therefore, the wearing of an afro was an abomination before God. That's period.

Anyway, before school started in 1968, I went to pick up my August check at the high school. I was wearing my first class afro which I had had cut in Chicago that summer. Mr. Hodges, the Principal, said, "Well, I guess that's our afro policy". Afros were in! The students loved me.

The next assault on my hair and person was the relaxer/perm, followed by the jeri curl and hundreds of other 'chemical warfare products'. Hair fries, sores and repair cycles. By the time your scalp heals, your hair was nappy again---it had gone back!. Today? Au naturel forever.

Norma Noble

THE YMCA LINCOLN PARK SENIOR CENTER WRITERS GROUP

DARLENE JOHNSON REID

Darlene Johnson Reid was born in Anadarko, Oklahoma in 1939, the 9th of 11 children. She later moved to Spencer, Oklahoma. Darlene is the mother of three wonderful children, Angelia, James Jr., and Michael with eleven grandchildren, fourteen great-grandchildren, and two great-great grand-children!

"I'm truly blessed of the Lord. May the words of my mouth and the meditations of my heart be acceptable unto God. That's my prayer."

Time/Chance

Winter is almost gone.
The beginning of spring is near.
Birds will be chirping
Beautiful melodies so dear.

As time goes by, she'll make a nest.
Her family, she'll have to feed
And have somewhere to rest.
Digging in the earth for food to eat.

Looking from side to side.
Listening for that awful CAT that causes defeat.
AWWW – There he is.

I'll just fly away
And come back again
Another time of the day.

No matter what.
It's a beautiful day.
I'll just sit and wait
'Til his head, down he lay.

Focus

Twenty eighteen is here.
What are your plans for the year?
Will you procrastinate? Hesitate?
Or will you accelerate without fear?

Twenty seventeen wasn't so bad.
It was a year you never had.
Did you choose to be happy
or be content to being sad?

Life isn't fair, there's always a dare.
Dare to forget, dare to regret.
This is your year, don't sit and fret.

Today, it's all you have.
Yesterday is gone.
Choose to be happy.
Stop singing that sad, old song.

Set your goals high,
Reach for the sky.
Be true to yourself.
Dare to fly high.

Words of Wisdom

Life owes you nothing!

It's what you make out of it. Yes, you weren't asked be born. You didn't have the opportunity to choose your family, your color of skin, appearance, your sisters and brothers, your place of living, or what others thought of you.

But now it's up to you! To be. To go. To accomplish everything you desire.

I was hung up on color, the lightest in the family. My size—skinny. My facial appearance—freckles. The house I lived in was poorly build, almost falling down. My clothes were hand-me-downs. I worried about what others thought of me.

Then I realized one day, life owes me nothing. We are all given a life to live, a mind, five senses, and a measure of faith. We have a conscience to know right from wrong, choices. Life is what I make it. By my choices, they determine where I go. Who I'll be. How smart I can be. My attitude on life.

Whatever the situation, or circumstances that come your way, you can do or not do. You can make the best of it or the worse. You can strive or give up. It's all up to you.

To blame someone else for your short comings isn't fair. We all must give an account for our deeds and works. And in the end, when you've done the best you can, go ahead.

Hold your head up high.

Choose to me happy. Like me.

GWENDOLYN HOOKS

Gwendolyn began her literary career with Can I Have A Pet?, an eight page, 36 word book that sold over 55,000 copies. She is now is the author of twenty-two published books.

Tiny Stitches – The Life of Medical Pioneer Vivien Thomas is a NAACP Outstanding Literary Work for Children winner, a Society of Children's Book Writers and Illustrators Crystal Kite winner for the Oklahoma and Texas region, the California Reading Association Eureka Silver Award for Nonfiction, Booklist starred review, and a NYC Reads 365, among other honors.

Her book, Block Party, is a 2017 Junior Library Guild Selection and made the Best Children's Books of the Year, 2018 Edition from Bank Street College of Education. Other awards include the Black Liberated Arts Center Ralph Ellison Literary Award 2017.

Gwendolyn facilitates the YMCA Lincoln Park Senior Center Writers Group.

Mama and Trees

Trees, sung by the Platters has found a permanent place in my heart. I've heard it many times, but wasn't until a few years ago that it became important to me. I still myself and smile at the world as I listen to the words.

The song is a musical version of the poem, *Trees*, by Joyce Kilmer. A few years before Mama's death, one of my sisters, said she asked her to find the song on her telephone. "You can do everything on that phone. Find it! I want to hear it." She found it and said Mama smiled all the way through it. I wondered what thoughts and memories came to mind.

It was the first time in many years, she mentioned a song that wasn't a church song. One of my daughters and my niece said that Mama recited the poem for them. They hadn't asked her. She just opened her mouth and out flowed Trees.

Where did she hear it or read it? Did she learn it in school? Mama never answered my questions to my satisfaction or to the satisfaction of my siblings. "I just know it." Was it a Mama secret not meant for daughters?

We played it at her funeral and now, it's one of my favorites. I'll continue to listen to it and think of Mama.

Be of Use

Before I was a writer, I taught math to middle schoolers. Seventh grade was my favorite grade to teach. They entered class with wide-eyed excitement. Still a little nervous, but willing to give school, math, and me, a chance.

Every morning, we had a moment of silence. I always prayed, "Let me be of use today." It helped me to remain calm and to look past first impressions, be patient, and question before condemning.

One of my girls put me to the test. Every day, she fell asleep half way through class. Every day, I woke her. Every day, I got a little more irritated. Finally, it occurred to me to ask why she was so sleepy. She said her mother worked at night and as the oldest, she had to feed, bathe, and put her younger brother and sister to bed. And they didn't want to go to bed. They kept her up late. That's why she was so sleepy in class. I made a point of standing by her desk as I talked about the day's lesson. That roused her. I gave her extra time to turn in her assignments.

She was twelve years old with an adult job. I wanted to ease her burden and be of use.

My Life as a Charm Bracelet

I don't own a charm bracelet. If I were to buy one, my bracelet would include...
• a charm that depicts my lady friends from our writing class. I would rub it when I was unsure and remember the strength these ladies represent.
• a sun. To remember in cloudy times, the sun will shine again—just give it time.
• one man, two girls, and one boy – my family. They are always there full of love and support.
• a sparkly blue stone to represent oceans, lakes, and swimming pools. Swimming is my favorite recreational activity.
• a book to represent my morning journal. I write my prayers and thoughts each day.
• a fingernail painted with sparkly purple polish. It would remind me of Bertil, who believes in taking time to treat yourself.
• tThe letter T to remind me our tomorrows are never guaranteed. Live life for today. And I will.

ADELLA LAVERN WILLIAMS SMITH

Adella grew up in West Town, a small African American community west of downtown Oklahoma City. She and her older brother, Wilbur, lost both parents by the time Adella was four years old. Grandmother Iona Harkey raised them.

What is now the Jesus House is the location of their West Town elementary school, Orchard Park. At Douglass High School, Adella played the violin in the orchestra. She also played the bugle in the Drum and Bugle Corps and in the band. Her cousin, James Butler owned a BBQ restaurant at NE 6th Street and Stonewall Avenue. Adella earned extra money working at the city-wide popular restaurant.

Adella graduated from Langston University with degrees in Social Sciences and Elementary Education. Besides leaving Langston University with her degrees, Adella also left with the love of her life, World War II veteran, Robert L. Smith. Robert attended Langston the same time as Adella. They met, fell in love and married. They had one child, Chequita Owens and one granddaughter.

Adella's widowed grandmother, Iona, taught them to share with others even if you don't have much. Train hoppers and hobos spread this sentiment threw out their community. They could always depend on Mrs. Harkey to have a hot breakfast waiting for them.

Adella's grandmother also believed in respecting your property, even if you were tenants and not owners. For Adella, it meant endless sweeping because there wasn't any grass!
She loved singing in the East Sixth Street Christian Church and photographing church and community events. Following her grandmother's lessons, she began Making Ends Meet, a food ministry for families in need.

Adella is a past president of her beloved sorority, Alpha Kappa Alpha.

What I Know for Sure

That the sun shines when it is its time to come up.
Nobody can tell you what to think.

A Holiday

A day for gathering friends together to visit and play games and talk to each other.
This is a time we share our wishes and dreams.
It's good to have friends that you feel that you can talk with and feel comfortable doing it.
Sharing how you feel and what you like to do with others helps us broaden our field of friends.

Love is in the Heart

Love is in the heart.
It's on the outside too.
It's also in the words we say
And in the deeds we do.
Love is an understanding heart.
I want you to know that I will do my part.
Just a note to let you know
I love you!

Words of Wisdom

I always speak to people. If they don't speak back, it's on them. But I've done my job.

My Passion

My passion is meeting new people.
I'm so glad to have met you.

Identical Twins

They say we seem alike
But I don't think that's true.
I am me and you are you!
You are me and I am you?

Come Play

Come play with me.
Now what shall we do?
Run, jump, climb a tree?
Or try a game that's new?
Maybe we'll sit and sing.
Read a book out loud.
Or should we go out and swing
And watch a big white cloud?
Shall we play a game?
Mold some clay?
Would it be the okay
if we just sat and looked all day?

by Adella Smith

The Men in My Life

My brother Wilbur Dean was one of the most important men in my life. My father died when I was four, so I never knew him. His brother, my Uncle Bill was active in my life. My Uncle Lemuel was very active in my life, too. He had two sons, but wanted a daughter.
He asked my grandmother if I could come and live with them. My grandmother said no. She was not sending me to Lawton so I could take care of my cousins! Uncle Lemuel married a second time and they had a daughter. He was so happy!

My brother was very protective of me. He was very talented. He had a nice singing voice and played the trumpet. He sang in the school chorus and was the student band director at Douglass.

Mammy's Butter Crisps

My grandmother's favorite cookies were Mammy's Butter Crisps. She made them from scratch. They were our favorite cookies. We would make them for special occasions. When our family gathered for holidays, we made them. They were special and the favorite cookies for the whole family.

Why Not More Peace

I can be a more perfect person. Sometimes, when I'm in a group, I notice there is a lack of respect toward some of the group's members. Some think they are in control of the group. I feel the need to say, "The group belongs to all of us. Each person has equal status. We are all special and should not forget to remember that."

Age

Age is nothing but a number. Being a certain age is not necessarily being a good person. Some people are not necessarily filled with joy at being a certain age.
I've finally learned to be grateful for whatever age I am. I try to be grateful for the friends I have. Some people are not blessed to have friends and relatives who care for them.
I try to remember the people who helped me and I will never forget them.

YMCA Lincoln Park Senior Center Writers Group

JOYCE TEASE JACKSON

A retired Art teacher from the Millwood and Oklahoma City Public Schools, Joyce Tease Jackson is currently developing her skills in acrylic, pastel painting and watercolor.She has done illustrations for seven childrens' books. Her works are included in The Black Oklahomans' History coloring Book.

She has participated in the John F. Kennedy Center for the Performing Arts' Seminar, "Artists as Educators:Presenting effective workshops for Teachers. She is the founder and Director of the Art Garden Studio; a community based outreach arts project. After school art classes are held in Community Schools; outreach workshops from the studio include Senior Adults and the Disabled. Also here they create Murals and decorative art on furniture! She is listed in the "Oklahoma Artists" Directory, published by the Melton Art Library.

Joyce enjoys reading and writing, and playing with her dog "Chico the Chihuaha", who inspires her to create.

Words of Wisdom

Words that I remember very early from my Mother were "Do unto others as you want them to do to you". You see my family was large, so I imagined this was a good way to curtail our behavior in order to have peace in a house with five children.

Another saying that comes to mind, I learned in the "brownies" club; " make new friends, but keep the old, one is silver and the other is gold"! But as I look back on my life, I realize that people come into our lives reasons, and seasons, which change continuously.

I've spent my life searching, and reading so many wise words in books,etc., however, the most important words I count on have been: "Trust in the Lord and lean not to your own understanding! Acknowledge Him in all your ways...."! These are the words that reassure, and encourage me, they cause me to remember and give me peace.

My Dog Max

I used to be afraid of dogs and lots of other things, but then I accepted an invitation to look at a dog, or so I thought, from one of my students. Well I gathered up my courage and took my neighboring teacher with me; partially because I needed actual support and also because she's had many dogs, and men and she knows how to train them both!

Well when I looked at all those cute little puppies, it was about a dozen of them squealing I just wanted all of them ! And then one tiny black one came close to me and of course I still had my inhibitions, but I picked him up and put this tiny creature close to me, and then he relaxed and put his little head on my chest. That just did it! It was as if he called my name and whispered " take me with you!" And with those beautiful brown marble eyes, you know which one I got!

I named him "Max"...... he was a cute 'short-legged' daschund, black with reddish brown accents. Max was quite a tough guy, always protecting and guarding the house so well, I didn't have all that fear anymore.

Joyce Tease Jackson

44

Joyce Tease Jackson

45

Joyce Tease Jackson

My Most Memorable Birth Year

It was a time of commitment and care for my family; My Mother and my Aunt both needed great help because of their health. This was a most challenging time of my life that I can remember; but I made peace with the "opportunity to serve, and love them". And as I suspected, I am so grateful that I did.

Well, because it was such a trying time, I actually felt that I deserved a unique, impressive Birthday celebration. The idea I had was to have a party for this 50th year, with a "male stripper"---something I've never experienced before! Usually for my birthday I'm taken to dinner or share a meal with someone. This year was to be my "new beginning" and the ending of 50 a whole years on the planet!

Needless to say, I came to my senses and stayed focused on being there for my Aunt and Mom; and I'm so grateful that I made that choice because my Aunt passed that year (the end of that month). It was such sweet sorrow, as she was 92, and to be there for her transition, helped me to remember what really matters, and that we all must come and go, and each part is so perfectly beautiful" that we can rejoice and praise God for a truly meaningful life!

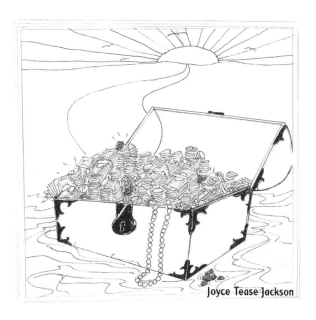

Joyce Tease Jackson

LYNNETTE M. HODGE

Lynnette M. Hodge is a poet, author and educator, nominated for State Poet Laureate of Oklahoma 2015-2016. Her poetry books are Keep Steppin': A Poetic Journey Part 1; Moving On: A Poetic Journey Part 2; and Poems Inspired by Love. They contain poems based on her memories and thoughts from childhood through adulthood. Her memoir, Still Steppin', includes writing done while in a memoir writing class for seniors.

Lynnette graduated from Douglass High School in Oklahoma City, OK, where she was class yearbook editor. She attended Lincoln University in Jefferson City, MO; then earned a B.S degree in Medical Technology at the Univ. Of Central OK (UCO) in Edmond, OK and became a Registered Medical Technologist. Later, she went to Vo-Tech school and was certified as an Electronic Imager/ Desktop Publisher by Oklahoma State Department of Vocational and Technical Education. She also took courses in writing and photography at OSU-OKC. She later returned to UCO and completed requirements to become a Certified Teacher in secondary education.

She wrote technical manuals while supervising a hospital microbiology lab   then worked in the production department of an award-winning daily business and legal newspaper. While teaching, she published a grade school newspaper, and later an adult student anthology. She was also Adult Learning Center Lead Technology Educator and webmaster.

She reads her poetry at celebrations, conferences, churches, nursing homes, at a senior citizens center and at library and museum open mic programs. Her hobbies are writing and making personalized crossword puzzles, cryptograms, calendars, books, collages, frameable poems, quotes; and tributes for family and friends. She has also published award-winning newsletters, made flyers, certificates, and fundraising items for non-profit organizations she supports. Her email address is lmhodge@ymail.com.

Describing Gratitude

One assignment we were given in our Memoir Writing Class for Seniors was to name something we are passionate about and describe how it looks, sounds, smells, tastes and feels. I chose to write about gratitude.

To me, gratitude looks like my mother smiling at me.

It sounds like a baby making those sweet indistinguishable murmurings that are so endearing.

It smells like the honeysuckle that grows in my back yard, blooming faithfully every year, requiring no maintenance; colorful and bright, sweet smelling; not overwhelming, but gentle and memorable _ a loving smell.

It tastes like frozen blueberries, red tart cherries and banana slices stirred with creamy home-made Greek style yogurt and spooned into a colored ice cream cone, and savored beyond satisfaction.

It feels like the creamy, fragrant concoction my youngest niece made for me to rub on my skin. Very soothing.

It makes me feel like raising my hands and looking up toward heaven to say:

"Thank you, Lord."

Why I Write

Writing is my hobby because I enjoy it.

I write to pay tribute to people who are or have been important in my life, including those who are deceased.

I write to leave something of myself behind.

I can express my feelings on issues in writing.

I can tell of events from my point of view.

Through writing I can elaborate on photos and images.

I can write about things that others may relate to and enjoy remembering.

I can entertain and sometimes make people laugh when I write.

Writing helps me to focus and see things more clearly.

I am at peace when I write. I forget about everything else and eliminate stress.

I can communicate with more people in writing than I can talk with in person.

I can make personalized gifts from my writing.

Sometimes I can't stop writing when ideas or memories pop into my head.

I write because I can. I'm blessed to be able to do it.

My Journey Toward Better Health

Personal health issues and the passing away of a former neighbor who was younger than I was, caused me to make lifestyle changes resulting in dramatic improvements in my medical conditions which included obesity, diabetes, high blood pressure, and high cholesterol levels. My family, friends and my physician were impressed with the results. I wrote about the experience in a series of reports entitled, What's Up, in which I shared the strategies and recipes I used.

My medical laboratory test results caused my physician to take me off medications. He congratulated me on improving my health, "reversing diabetes", lowering my blood pressure, losing weight and having lower blood cholesterol levels.

Friends wanted to know what I was eating while I made these improvements. Some commented on my healthier-looking skin. They were especially interested in knowing how I "reversed diabetes". I started trying to explain everything in an email, but that wasn't enough. Menus, recipes and other information needed to be included. And since improving health is a continuous process, there's always something new to be learned about it. I still educate myself by reading articles on healthy living.

What I accomplished hasn't been that difficult. I make occasional exceptions to my new routines, but I know how important my health is, so I usually do the right things. I sometimes eat out, or sample decadent dessert on special occasions, but not nearly as often as I did before.

Though I worked in healthcare for many years, I've had health issues off and on all my life. My neighbor's death made me determined to get healthier, and I did.

QUEEN ESTER SATTIEWHITE

Queen Esther Sattiewhite is an east Texas lady from Rusk County. She attended Colcord High School and stays in contact with her classmates.

She has been a business woman operating her own day care center in the Creston Hills section of Oklahoma City, Queen Day Care.

Queen Esther married Marvelus Sattiewhite, the love of her life. They raised five children, Jaurene, Sharon, Marcelle, Marvelus, and Patrina. Now that they are adults, she has plenty of time to devote to her beautiful flowers and the peacocks who love them.

Queen Esther and her family have been faithful members of Eastside Church of Christ for more than 50 years.

My Family

I would go to Denver to visit my daughter, Jaurene and my cousin, Peggy. I would go up to the mountain. I would ride the bus. I'd rather go up on the bus. I would be afraid to ride in a car. While I'm there, we would go shopping and sightseeing. On Sunday, we would go to church. My daughter sings. She has a beautiful voice. All of my four daughters sang in Millwood's choirs. They were in the band. My only son, Marvelus II played the bass drum at Millwood High School and two of my daughters ,Patrina and Jaurene, were majorettes at Millwood.

Learning to Drive

My mother ran into a tree learning how to drive. I didn't let it stop me from learning. Our truck was a stick shift. My brother, Eddie was a year younger than me and he was driving when he was about 12. We would drive to Fort Worth before I had a license. When we got as far as Dallas about 200 miles away, I let him have the driver seat. I also drove to school and to the grocery store. All my classmates and friends learned how to drive early.

My Mother

I was reminded of my mother, Gracie Tutt in the days when she was young. She went to church with her parents. They lived in the country.

When we were growing up in the country in east Texas, we would gather some greens, squash, lettuce, corn, beans, tomatoes, and potatoes, yams, and onions from their garden to cook in the Sunday meal. We would pick grapes, blackberries to make a blackberry cobbler. Mother made grape jelly. My parents grew ribbon cane and sugar can to make syrup. I remember eating corn bread and buttermilk.

We would kill hogs on cold days. We had a creek that ran through our land that Mother would fish.

Lord, forgive me for my sins. I went to a club on Friday nights. I really enjoyed myself. We had beef, chicken, green beans, potatoes, rolls, cheese cake, and ice tea. They had a nice band and I danced so much, my hair went back!

Growing up in Texas

My sister and I dressed alike. Like Easter every day. My hair was thick and coal black. Shirley Temple curls. Every summer vacation, I spent with my father in Fort Worth, Texas. He worked in Fort Worth at Berl's Mill. He would send money and beautiful clothes. I always liked to dress and dance.

I worked at Peter Smith Hospital as a nurse aid. Then I decided to go to beauty school. I moved to Fort Worth with my father. I started going to Mr. Terrell Cosmetology Beauty College in 1953. After I finished my one thousand hours I went to Austin, Texas to take the State Boards. I passed and received my cosmetology license and started to work at Amenda Street Beauty Shop in Fort Worth, Texas.

I took the state boards in Austin, Texas. Relaxer, neutralized perms—I can do it all. Worked at white shop. They tipped me big.

Marvelous

I graduated from high school in east Texas, on Garrison Route and went to Concord School from elementary through high school. I graduated in 1953. I was engaged to marry Z B Lewis. We got our blood test, but Mama would not give her permission for us to marry. It took me a long time to forget about him. Mother sent me to Fort Worth to forget him. Then I met Marvelous Sattiewhite. He was a city boy. I was from the country. Marvelous was ready to get married. He fell in love with me when he first met me. He dressed cool. He left his girlfriend for me. She was a light skinned girl. I guess he loved black skinned girls. We got engaged and I married Marvelous in July 1953. My husband worked for 53 years at FAA.

What's So Great about the Age I Am Today?

I am so proud to be my age today. I thank Heavenly Father for his blessings and his love to let me live on this earth for so many years. I've stayed by myself for 12 years. I'm not afraid. I ask the Lord to give me courage and strength for every step of the way. The Lord has blessed me with four children, a home, and a way to travel. I have 12 grandchildren and six great grandchildren.

I take nothing for granted. For when you do, the joy of enjoying is lessened for you.
Today I valued the beauty of the changing seasons. Whatever time of year, there is evidence that God is near. You'll find when you smile, your day will be brighter.

Spring Summer Fall Winter

I like spring and the beautiful flowers blooming. I like working in my garden, setting out flowers. And I like the peacocks that visit my flowers.

Summer is too hot for me and I stay inside. We take family vacations during the summer.

Fall is when the flowers begin to die. I pick up pecans and persimmons in my yard.

At the start of winter, I pull out my warm clothes.

Late

I used to be on time all the time. But since my husband passed, I take my time to get ready to go to church. I'm usually late for Sunday School. When my husband was living, I would be on time. He was never late.

If I had to go somewhere at a certain time, I would be on time. My daughter started taking me with her on different occasions, like pedicures, lunch, and dinner.

Sometimes, I pick up my friends when we are going out. They don't drive anymore. I try to be on time.

My Prayer

Faith for our Father
Always care in God
Thoughtfulness
Everlasting Lord
Righteousness,
He taught me.

Center Director
**YMCA LINCOLN PARK
SENIOR CENTER**

DONNELL DAVIS

ACKNOWLEDGEMENTS

Thank you to...

Donnell Davis, for providing a meeting place for our group and her continuing support and encouragement,

Bill Broiles, photographer

Jillian Coker, All Access Arts Director,

Nic Caudle, All Access Arts Assistant,

All Access Arts – Arts Council Oklahoma City, and the

YMCA of Greater Oklahoma City.

A special thank you to our families and friends who inspired us to cherish and record our memories.

CREDITS

Thank you to the photographers at Pixabay.com, who graciously share their work and their art to make projects like this possible.

Marla Jones
Book creator and designer

To purchase additional copies of this book, contact:

Doodle and Peck Publishing
P.O. Box 852105
Yukon, OK 73085

(405) 354-7422

www.doodleandpeck.com

Doodle and Peck

PUBLISHING

CPSIA information can be obtained
at www.ICGtesting.com
Printed in the USA
BVHW02n1125310718
523164BV00003B/6/P